"The poems in Smith's collection *Baltimore Sons* aim to make sense of suffering. With razor-sharp language that balances witness and wound, Smith recounts the past and aftermath of three generations of sons struggling to navigate life on the fringes of society. Filled with the volatile heat of a loaded gun, these poems astound and transform us. *Baltimore Sons* grounds us in truth and sorrow echoing those too familiar entanglements of American life—class, race, and violence. Yet, in the spirit of Lucille Clifton, there's the quiet undertow of survival celebrated within."

CRYSTAL SIMONE SMITH, author of *Dark Testament*

"'We are all targets. / We are all unsafe,' Dean Smith writes in this plain spoken collection that unflinchingly explores the nation's gun culture— what it offers and what it takes away. Always the threat of violence looms among these lines, but also beauty, love, and even joy. Even hope."

GERRY LAFEMINA, author of *Graffiti Heart*

"Dean Smith's *Baltimore Sons* is the kind of walk down memory lane that makes you laugh and cry, that wakes you in the middle of the night, unsettled. Fathers and sons, drunkards and guns, love and loss; attempts to find comfort and a sense of belonging in sports, when a sense of true family fails. You don't have to be a Baltimorean of early 1960s vintage (though, full disclosure, I am) to appreciate this fierce and moving collection. Like Smith, true enough, 'the bird and the blue horseshoe' remain 'carved into my soul.' Carved even more deeply, though: the image of a mother on her deathbed, 'ruby beads / from a transfusion' dripping. 'Why do roses die?' Why indeed, other than to be reborn in these tough, spare, and ultimately grace-filled poems."

MOIRA EGAN, author of *Synaesthesium*

"The word 'home' conjures warmth and domesticity, a good life worth fighting for. But in *Baltimore Sons*, home is more complex: a landscape of harrowing childhood memories set against a city wracked by gun violence, drugs, and riots. To navigate such a place—and to lovingly raise a family in the midst of chaos—is today's almost insurmountable problem. This is why we need a poet like Dean Smith, who, if not fully reconciling love and damage, charts a clear-eyed path for those who long to be at home in the world with a survivor's sense of grace, acceptance, and wisdom."

RICHARD JONES, editor of *Poetry East*

"In *Baltimore Sons*, the city rises inside the breath of memories that are the history of a place. In Smith's terse language, Baltimore is the heart of the nation, containing its hopes and wrecked dreams, drawing them along the persistent presence of our tragic bonding with drugs, guns, and violence. His poems give a deftness in bones that sing songs of the commonality of loss in a great city, a loss that the poet carves alongside a faith in the idea that it could still become a haven for dreamers of hope and change."

AFAA M. WEAVER, author of *Spirit Boxing*

"So many astonishing faces and details haunt these poems. They are so masterfully executed, that even while one admires their virtuosity, one is rushing ahead to read more. The whole is beautifully arranged into what amounts to a kind of memoir in poems by a man who cares deeply for others, carries the weight of history on his shoulders—a citizen, and father, a true son of Baltimore. Bursting with vitality, truth, and gunfire, it's a succinctly relevant American book."

ALAN KAUFMAN, *editor of The Outlaw Bible of American Poetry*

"*Baltimore Sons* is a wounded, hopeful promise to a city, the pages a stage for heroes, victims, survivors and—in honor of their losses—an argument for a better future, seen through the poet's story. There is a shimmering nostalgia, arrested for a moment of greatness under a spiraling football in the klieg lights, and there is the raw, useless loss in the electric glare of a restaurant, a chef gunned down in a robbery on his way to a midnight shift. Notes taped to poles and diner windows call out the city's fallen, the random casualties fueled by poverty and crime."

BRUCE CRAVEN, author of *Win or Die: Leadership Secrets from Game of Thrones*

BALTIMORE SONS

DEAN BARTOLI SMITH

STILL
HOUSE
PRESS

FAIRFAX, VIRGINIA

All inquiries may be directed to:
    Stillhouse Press
    4400 University Drive, 3E4
    Fairfax, VA 22030
    www.stillhousepress.org

Stillhouse Press is an independent, student and alumni-run
nonprofit press based out of Northern Virginia and established in
collaboration with the Fall for the Book festival.

Library of Congress Control Number: 2021935408
ISBN-13: 978-1-945233-12-8

Interior Layout: Meghan McNamara
Cover Design: Scott Levine
Cover Art: Stephen Reichert

PART I

PART II

FOR MARY JULIA, QUINN,
AND ALL THE CITY'S CHILDREN

PART I

SIX SHOOTERS

My mother's
first love gave me
my first toy guns.

Nickel-plated Colt .45s,
mother-of-pearl grips,
a leather holster.

Before joining the Marines,
Mickey proposed;
my mother would flash his ring.

"I almost was your father,"
he tells me every time I see him.
He's still in love with her.

My father vowed to watch over
his best friend's fiancée,
then moved in for the kill.

Dad pulled his trigger first.
Mom gave back the ring.
I was born.

ALI

I met my first poet
in second grade
at the bus stop

taking sides before the fight
of the century

Joe Frazier versus
Muhammed Ali

float like a butterfly
sting like a bee

how could you not follow him
into the ring after that couplet

alone
taunting the other side

with his voice

Joe Frazier can't hit what
Joe Frazier can't see

and when Smokin' Joe
broke the poet's jaw,
I cried myself to sleep.

CASH FOR GUNS, 1975

Sunday morning, bitter cold—
my father turned in
the Remington 700 deer rifle
he'd won selling spark plugs
in an Esso sales contest.

Before the divorce, I'd sneak
into my parent's closet, unzip
the rawhide sleeve and lift
the rifle out. Peering
through the scope,

I aimed the heavy gun
at the floor, pulled the trigger.

Dad was behind
on his child support.
He needed fifty bucks
for food. I watched him walk
slowly to the police station,
cradling the rifle like a son.

OUTLAW

I twirled a six-gun
at the crab feast,
pointed it at
the candy-striped
mid-section
of Aunt Bernice
holding court
in her lawn chair.
"Give me that
damn thing,"
she said,
and yanked it
out of my hand,
tearing the skin
off my trigger finger.
"I'll teach you to
point a gun at me."
She stuffed
the silver pistol
into her shiny
black pocketbook
and then sipped her
Cutty Sark on the rocks.

"Don't you come crying to me, boy."

THE STICKUP

I pulled a gun on my father
during my last year of college

(a few weeks before, I'd blacked out
on mushrooms and tequila

behind the wheel, avoiding
a head-on collision).

My friend Bob lent me
the .45 with an ivory pistol grip

for protection against
a string of robberies in the area.

I pointed it at my father.
Dad backed away, his hands

in front of his face.
The silver barrel shone

under a Virginia moon.
Both of us drunk.

I gave it to him like
it was nothing at all.

"It's okay," I said.
"The gun's not loaded."

EMPTY THE CHAMBER

Dad keeps a loaded .357 Magnum
on top of his dresser. At the firing range,
he wipes drug dealers off streets,
guns down intruders.

My father shows me paper targets riddled
with holes—obliterated faces and hearts.
He grew up in Baltimore; he will make
someone pay for its ruin.

I've felt his anger on my skin. I know,
in real life, he will not hesitate.
He hears things at night, crouches
in boxer shorts, points

his weapon with both hands
at shadows from streetlamps.
"Feel the weight," he says.
I empty the chambers, run

bullets through my fingers,
squeeze the trigger once,
hand back the gun.

AT THE BEL-LOC DINER

The moment I knew my father loved me
occurred a few weeks after I left my wife.
We both ordered the breakfast special,
two eggs over easy, hash browns,
scrapple, and black coffee
on a bright summer morning.
He wore sunglasses in the booth,
pretended to read the sports page.
"It's a good thing you didn't have
children," he said, and glanced
out the window. From the angle
of the sun, I could see his eyes
behind the lenses, welling up
as he drifted to nights
spent alone in this diner,
single again, with a hot
roast beef sandwich,
reading the sports page—
while my brother and I
slept in the bedroom
across town, where he
used to tuck us in.

PISTOL RANGE

My father grits his teeth,
braces himself, earplugs
snug in their sockets:

Fire spurts from the nozzle,
bullets rip through paper,
sweat beads under his goggles:

Today, he takes the law
into his own hands.
Not a policeman or a soldier,

but a disgruntled son
out for revenge. He utters
a list of citations against a father

who guzzled money saved
for Christmas presents,
who cheated on his mother

as she lay dying of lung cancer.
He kills him over and over,
enjoying every moment.

MY FATHER'S TRAINS

He bequeaths to me all the train gardens
he has ever constructed (and each of the engines
that whistled through them): the Zephyr,
Meteor, and Crescent City Flyer,
all the Pullman cars, cabooses, and freighters
rolling across mint condition track
on an immaculate platform past
ballfields and parks, war memorials,
miniature churches, fire stations, billboards
hawking Norelco and National Bohemian,
a double-feature at the drive-in playing
The Guns of Navarone and *The Dirty Dozen,*
beneath elevated trestles and mountain tunnels,
through valleys with lakes reflecting
blue skies of endless prosperity,
while passengers note freshly dug graves
made with coffee grounds, motorized skaters,
squad cars, and patrol officers glued to the streets.

Trains never crash in his imaginary town,
no citizen mugged, beaten, or carjacked—
a direct result of every household bearing
a .357 Magnum, bullets included, handed out
in D-Day Park or General Patton Playground.
He's erected monuments to Confederate generals,
their swords raised, their horses rearing up into battle
alongside all the white children, each trained—
in this imaginary town—at an early age to handle a gun
like the one I will discover in a shoe box long after he's gone,

mistaking its barrel for an old locomotive until I lift it out, knowing it's loaded.

ORDNANCE

At Sunny's Surplus, I wore gas masks,
ammo belts, helmets wrapped in camouflage.
Crawling between the aisles, I aimed

a wooden rifle at the ankles of customers.
Pop-pop said I could pick one item:
a gas mask, compass, canteen.

Bayonets and machetes were off limits—
the Marine saber, encased in glass
at the check-out counter, a non-starter.

I chose a .50 caliber round of dummy ammo
and pretended it was a rocket headed for the moon.

I had no idea that this bullet—twice the length
of my middle finger—could shear a man in half.

BIG BOY

On Saturday afternoons, Queenie and I would watch Walter Brennan in *The Guns of Will Sonnet* ride west with his grandson to find the father. We loved the gunslingers—Mitchum, Widmark, and Wayne, gunning each other down.

Now she's bald and on morphine, her last request: a crab cake. "Get your gun, boy," she told my father from her hospital bed. "We're busting out tonight." She tore away the covers and started to roll out.

"That will never happen to me," says my father. He points a forefinger to his temple like the barrel of a pistol. He promises me his gun will cure him of any terminal illness.

UNSELD

He soft-tossed the ball
against the backboard,

jumped up, snared it
with both hands,

spun around in the air
at six-foot-seven, launched

an outlet pass high above the court
to hit the opposite glass—

one time breaking a light
on the suspended scoreboard.

The smallest center in the NBA,
wide as a doorframe, strong,

with fury embedded in his gaze,
he could barely dunk the ball,

but he defended the seven-footer
Kareem Abdul-Jabbar better

than anyone—by nudging him
with his knees, stepping on his feet.

He called me down in front
of the whole camp to try

and take the ball from him.
Each time I reached in,

his elbow grazed
the corner of my eye.

"I hate point guards,"
he said.

He tucked me in after lights out
like a father would do.

BALTIMORE

Pop-pop bragged
about the sawn-off shotgun
he kept in his lap
while driving a potato chip truck
in case anyone got funny with him
during the riots of '68.

He showed me his freshly oiled .45,
loaded, in a jewelry box for protection.
He won it in a craps game.

On the way into the city for Sno Balls,
he reached under the front seat
and pulled out a lacquered baton—
the handle wrapped in electrical tape,
the shiny oak coated in polyurethane,
a cowhide loop for swinging.

He raised the nightstick toward me
at a stoplight and lightly tapped my shoulder.
It scared the hell out of me.

CAP GUNS

for T.J. Sellari

We played *Gunsmoke,*
took turns as Festus

and Marshall Dillon twirling
mother-of-pearl Colt .45s

down Northwood Drive,
fast becoming outlaws

with bandanas over our mouths,
yelling, "This is a stickup!"

Brendan and I, officers
Reed and Malloy

from *Adam-12,*
pointing die cast .38s

across the hoods
of imaginary squad cars

yelling "Hold it!" and "Come out
with your hands up!"

We knew back then not to stray
too far down the alley

and soon grew tired
of shooting blanks.

We unbuckled our holsters,
bursting rounds on creek stones

rock against rock
until the raised bump

on the red strip
exploded the whiff

of spent caps
into memory.

SIDEARM

Playing with Tonka trucks
under the dining room table,
I asked Mom, "Can you bring

me someone to play with?"
Maybe Dad would come
home earlier.

I watched her limp up
the driveway nine months later:
arms as empty as winter grass.

My brother spent his first
two months in an oxygen tent.
Dad left when he could breathe easier.

She worked two jobs
to feed us.

HOWITZER

My brother and I killed each other, played one-on-one tackle football in the snow, drank hot chocolate while clothes tumbled slowly in the dryer, watched *Mannix* and *The Cisco Kid* and periodically expressed our love for one another by punching each other in the face like Rock 'Em Sock 'Em Robots, chased the Good Humor man on choppers with banana seats, read *Curious George* and *Where the Wild Things Are*, zoomed Hot Wheels cars, pitched baseball cards, pelted school buses with snowballs, drove golf carts into a lake, decapitated hydrangea with seven irons, smoked joints and read Xaviera Hollander's *The Happy Hooker* by flashlight in the tree fort, destroyed mailboxes, stole from liquor cabinets, guzzled Smirnoff and Inglenook, flung toilet paper into trees, played with matches, soaped windows, smashed pumpkins, threw tomatoes, swam all day until the chlorine burned our eyes, watched game shows like *Match Game 74* and cranked up 45s like "Don't Mess Around with Jim" and "Long Cool Woman in a Black Dress" as we lay on shag carpet and obsessed over ads on the back covers of comic books for Daisy Rifles and German Lugers, officially banned by our parents, so instead we sprayed bullets with plastic Tommy Guns, Winchesters, M16s, .38 pistols, derringers, and Colt 45s, strafing redcoats, Apaches, Viet Cong, and Nazis in every battle—my brother and I, the undisputed champions of the world.

PURE SHOOTER

I watched him spin
a basketball on his index finger
and lift it over the rim,
still twirling into the net:
the first memory of my father
hypnotized me forever,
wanting to spin the ball
on my finger
and shoot like him.
He learned to play
with a rubber balloon
and a trashcan in a Baltimore
back alley, carrying groceries
for a dime, selling newspapers.
He picked my mother's heart
clean down the ocean
and they lasted seven years
before he left to pursue
his basketball dream.

I'm half-Italian, half-Irish,
coming from hubcap stealers
and horse thieves,
narcissists and nuns,
a natural bipolarism.

He taught me to move
without the ball—
shoot from anywhere.

ASSASSIN SONNET

She confessed to almost ending my life,
one month into '63. I clung to her
insides through a makeshift St. Patrick's Day
wedding, an insult to her Neapolitan
family, and she nearly bled out after
my birth, wandered the corridors
of a shit-show hospital, the blood
on her feat smearing a law school dream,
lost and alone, an AWOL Pietà.
She spent half a life killing for me,
clutching my sock from the balcony
as I stopped to look back on my way to school,
her long black hair against a white nightgown,
her warrior gaze—murderous, beautiful.

MEETING ARCHIE CLARK AT THE FLAMING PIT

I recognized Archie Clark
one night while having fried shrimp
with my mother at
Ordell Braase's Flaming Pit.

Clark played shooting guard
for the Baltimore Bullets,
replacing Earl "The Pearl" Monroe,
recently traded to the Knicks.

He sat down at our table,
gave me his phone number,
and told me to call him when I
wanted to play basketball.

A few weeks later,
I called from a pay phone
at the gym where my friends
and I were playing hoops.

He answered and I could hear music
and a woman's laughter
in the background.
He said to call back another time.

On the court, Tolly Nicklas
said the only reason Archie
gave me his number
was so he could fuck my mother—

"She likes to sleep with Black guys."
I punched him in the face.
He gave me a black eye.
I never called Archie again.

MISS MASON

Yvonne ate us alive for breakfast, lunch, and dinner.
She served pork chops, barbecue, fried chicken,
BLTs, Y-ghetti with meat sauce, and a mean streak
that might get you a brick of frozen grits and jalapeños
for saying the wrong thing. She banged pots to wake us
as the fragrance of bacon, eggs, and toast wafted up
through the staircase, mopping away last night's
haul of Tequila and Labatt Blue. She belonged
to the Order of the Eastern Star, raised us
into men with a steak knife that dared
our frightened tongues to speak.

MEMORIAL STADIUM

for Dr. Abdul Jamaludeen

A long fly ball to deep left field
and a deafening roar on summer nights
heard as far away as Hampden and Putty Hill,
when my life hung on every pitch
through a Zenith transistor,
and on Saturday afternoons, I burst
through turnstiles toward an outfield
expanse illumined with promise
first glimpsed through the portal
of the section ramp as we approached
with rosaries in our pockets
and an expectation of championships,
taking me far away from a broken home.
I sat in the bleachers
with tugboat captains, steel workers, and cab drivers
with their hard-earned, dirt-smudged
dollar bills now forked over for peanuts
eaten in their shells and watery Coca-Cola
in wax cups nibbled on into the late innings
when games got close, on wooden benches,
our fingers laden with splinters on tankard night.
The Orioles eked out victories in bushels,
with all of us part of a makeshift family,
and we loved each other from all over town
in "The World's Largest Outdoor Insane Asylum,"
huddled together in the bitter December air
to watch the Colts rise on their back hooves
in response to a bestial din boiling over:
a doomed and obsessive love affair
between a city and its heroes

created an unbroken family
of Black and white stars:
Jim Parker and Johnny U.,
Eddie Murray and Cal Ripken,
Frank and Brooks Robinson.
More than champions, they were
our Baltimore fathers and brothers and sons
in a wild and badass cauldron of love—
the bird and the blue horseshoe
carved into my soul.
Black and white fans cheered side-by-side,
equally, for all players on that field
and rose to their feet every time
Big Daddy Lipscomb chased after a ball carrier,
the entire stadium thundering: "Get 'em, Big Daddy.
Get 'em, Big Daddy. Get 'em, Big Daddy."
The city ripped its own heart out
by demolishing the rumbling brick
mastodon, leaving us entombed there
with the glory of our deeds eclipsed
by stabbings and drive-by shootings,
gangs and drug lords, needles in arteries,
children gunned down while playing
on their porches, joining the ghosts
of our heroes, visions of Big Daddy
roaming the gridiron, his cleat marks
covered by shell casings, chalk outlines,
blood stains across a city of vacant stares
in need of a last-second Unitas comeback.

SPORTSWRITER

Hartzell's cartoon bird
on the front page of the *Sun*
taught me to read—
"Birds *edge* Bosox" or
"Orioles *drub* Twins."

My team *routed*,
pummeled, *crushed*,
and *bombed* opponents—
just like the B-52s
in the headlines.

Years later, in smoke-laden
hallways and shibeens,
the inquisitive eyes
of Jiminy Cricket
peered over horned rims,
grilled my father
for answers.

Others had names
like Tanton, Henneman,
and Bill Free, who dressed
in the style of Superfly
or Charles O. Finley.

"Nobody cares about
the labor pains, just the baby,"
my father told them

on the record. "That referee
is a gutless son-of-a bitch."

I composed lines
after every game—
imagining myself
in the locker room—
from a stool
in the Owl Bar,
telling strangers
I wrote sports
for the *Sun*.

But I wasn't a writer
or a coach's son
when I looked
in the mirror
at my audience
of one—
drunk once again.

BOWMAN

Vietnam vet, bullets
zipping past his ears
in the jungle,

became an overnight security guard
at the *Baltimore Afro-American*.
He liked to cook.

After midnight, on his way
to work, he stopped at Yau's
Carry Out on Greenmount

for a plate of his usual
pork ya ka mein,
eating only the egg

and noodles, when the boys
came in like bandits from a Western:
kerchiefs over their mouths,

robbing a saloon, and a scuffle
ensued. One kid
put a bullet in his chest

without a second
thought, murdering
a great chef

who gave generous
portions, and never stayed
angry at anyone.

His sheeted body
in the street
still haunts me.

TRASH NIGHT, GUILFORD

At night, by stars: an exchange
of gunfire up the road,

where Pop-pop took shots
of Imperial and Schlitz,

disrupting a quiet walk to the gardens.
A rust-red fox darts from the bushes,

smirking as he crosses—
as if he knows exactly where

the bones are buried.
My pace quickens

as the No. 11 bus to Canton
rounds the corner like Jim Parker

and gone are the days of the Fusting boys
playing tackle on an empty lot

all afternoon disguised as Unitas,
Berry, and Moore.

I think of brandishing an iron
in my hometown and linger

near the manse of Ogden Nash—
now patrolled by Baskerville hounds;

the city's gone to the dogs.
Those endless spans of tulip bulbs

go a long way to assuage the fears
and warm the azure blood

of a Codfish Cult whose time has passed.
Sleepless in a sunken park, the barred owl hoots

its warning to my children, awake in their beds,
terrified "the robbers" will come again.

BALTIMORE SONS

Three-hundred and forty-three
people murdered last year
in Baltimore[1],

mostly with handguns,
the weapon of choice,
obtained illegally,

almost all victims and suspects
previously arrested,
mostly gang members

in drug crews using
guns on rival
gang members,

muscling in on
or defending turf
or retaliating for past acts,

the average victim
with eleven arrests,
the average suspect,

nine, no motive
for half of the killings,
mostly Black, mostly male,

mostly drug-related,
mostly between
18 and 34, killed outdoors,

more than half shot in the head,
thirteen of them
children,

in a city known for crab cakes,
marble steps, and the deadliness
of its shootings.

_____

[1] Murder statistics from the *Baltimore Sun*, December 27, 2017.

MCKENZIE

Killed by a stray bullet
on her front porch

during a drive-by
gun battle at sunset

while playing with dolls,
McKenzie Elliot, age three,

could count to 30 and knew
her ABCs in a neighborhood
where no one dared snitch.

It took five years to find the shooter
in a neighborhood that used to be
full of baseball fans in the summer,
that used to be joyous and exuberant
before the stadium was torn down—

a little girl died and was buried
in a small pink coffin.

STATION NORTH

I look out from a rooftop
                    six stories up
on Friday nights
    after my shift

and can do nothing but hope
the children
                    stay safe
in their rowhomes tonight,
next to burned-out shells
and vacants,

protected by bullet-strafed doors.

Next week,
                    the coroner
will inspect a new shipment

of ventilated sheaths—
        an endless conveyor belt
of Black bodies served up to the game; he'll notice

that the gunshot wounds

            on their delicate corpses

resemble miniature potholes

and make a small note
about the bullet that entered the chest
             of victim 248

and no one cares
about the murders

because   *"It's not*
             in my neighborhood"

and kids get killed,
caught in crossfires,
executed on corners,
dumped on lawns.

Every night the television
will ask,

     "Do you know
where your children are?"

His dead body, sheeted

in the street, immaculate
Nike LeBrons protruding like
an eternal dream.

BULLET FRAGMENTS

Gunfire at midnight
outside my window:
not the usual gang volleys
but two shots: definitive, full stops.

I see a boy facedown in the street
in a Redskins jersey,
a defensive back beaten deep
for a touchdown.

No sirens swirling lights
or squad cars, just a flashlight
and the hum of an ambulance
idling for pickup and delivery.

"Don't believe what they say,
you were a good son to me,"
his mother wrote on a flyer
tacked to a maple.

I recognized the snapshot
from his twentieth birthday.
Our brief exchange occurred
on my way home from Lautrec

or the Mambo Room and consisted
of a nod and a "no thanks"
when he offered me "rock."
At the base of the tree,

his memorial grows: photos
curled under rose petals, bottles
of Rémy Martin drained in his honor—
a soldier's goodbye.

RIOTS

No gunshots or sirens
before supper that night

in Little Italy after the melee
and you kept repeating

it's too quiet in the back seat,
afraid for your life,

hatred gusting around you
and your lower lip

tinged blue
like when I cradled

you moments after birth,
too angry to breathe.

Trembling in the seatbelt,
you said, *It's not safe*

out there. Daddy,
don't make me go.

Footage from the night before
ran through your eight-year-old

mind—a boy smashing
the back window

of a police car,
storefronts exploding,

a microburst tearing
across the street

outside the ballpark.
I told you the riots were over.

Choppers scanned alleyways
with searchlights.

Chunks of plate glass
in mounds like cooler ice.

I lied to you that it was safe
to come out because

you'll never know
how much I love this city,

every inch of its hard-up streets,
its finger-scraped mustard

from backfins, and splinters
from bleachers seats

when Eddie Murray stepped
to the plate, how most days

I still dream of running
underneath a Johnny Unitas

touchdown pass to feel
that roar in the upper deck

on the back of my neck,
and how I carry with me

the taste of a chocolate Sno Ball
topped with marshmallow,

and an image of the harbor
at dusk from Federal Hill

with the ruby letters
of "Domino Sugar" blinking

into an electric indigo sky.
But this would never

be your hometown.
You, my son, knew too much

about a corner boy
past his prime

like David Simon's
Bodie Broadus:

too long in the game,
in the wrong place

for a "rough ride"
downtown at 8 a.m.

You knew that no one
cradled him on the steel

floor of a paddy wagon,
tossed around, unresponsive

like so many other dead
boys littered across the city

in car trunks, on front lawns,
in dumpsters, and you felt anger

simmering on all sides like the lid
of a crab pot boiling over.

The next day, a phalanx of police
crouched like sitting ducks

as bricks hammered their shields,
a pharmacy looted and torched,

an unfinished nursing home
burned to the ground.

I'm not hungry. Daddy,
please take me home.

PART II

FATHERHOOD

He sprinted toward the curb
during rush hour and launched
a three-pointer from the Parker-Gray
housing project at my open sunroof.

The half-brick traveled through the air
with a shooter's arc and backspin
and I braced myself for impact
when it slammed next to my head

against the driver's side window
a little short of the opening and somehow
didn't shatter glass into my face
a few days after the birth of my son.

I swerved into the next lane, still alive,
with the kid in the corner of my eye
on a fast break and I turned onto his street
and started to chase him down;

then I remembered that my baby boy—
who had emerged early from the womb
so angry he'd forgotten to breathe,
turning blue, narrowly avoiding

intensive care—needed me to be alive,
and that half-brick, a few inches lower,
would've fractured my skull,
leaving him without a father.

GWENDOLYN AND FREDDIE

She saw his life end
before he was born
in the alley behind her house

where Black blood
seeped into the cracks
of concrete and crab grass:

young guns just like Freddie
murdered in Chicago no different
than in his hometown.

He liked slinging dope
past his shelf life on the corner,
a new father at twenty-five

making some extra scratch
but not enough to keep the boy
alive on the front porch

when it was showtime
and she knew how fast
the street ran in her own veins—

How she longed to *strut*
the streets with paint
on her face, witnessing

his "rough ride" downtown
after police bent him to the ground
and put a knee in his back,

then dragged him across
the cleated steel innards
of a paddy wagon, his last breaths

in her muscular arms
as she delivered routine lines
in a deep, god-laced timbre

as they drove him away:
He real cool.
He die soon.

———

The italics in stanza 7 come from "a song in the front yard" by Gwendolyn Brooks.
The italics in the final stanza are derived from "We Real Cool" (also by Brooks).

READING JAMES BALDWIN ON
ELECTION DAY IN CHARLESTON

Your voice rises
into molasses-laden air

under a canopy of palmettos
firing salvos into my soul.

I sit in the park by the Old Citadel,
built to quell slave revolts—

now a pink castle called
Embassy Suites, its lobby

arrayed in ceiling fans
and ferns, plantation-style.

The "blood-stained banner"
of the South unfurls its blue sautoir,

those hideous bars of rejection
embraced by the blinkered

and deadly dumb among us
who amass guns like grocery items

to feed new rebellions. The Church
of Mother Emanuel is locked up:

now a fortress against another invasion,
her cross off-plumb, those bodies still

turned to their god studying a book
in prayer like those bodies

in the synagogue turned to their god,
studying a book in prayer

where bullets become
crucifixion nails.

JOY RIDE

You gunned the engine
one hundred miles an hour
down Ocean Highway

in your royal blue '58 Thunderbird
while your friends "creamed with excitement"
and popped a cork in the back seat

and told you not to sweat being late,
that the rhythm method odds
were in your favor because

it was your first time. Unable
to breathe when the test
came back, your life skidded

to a stop in a used car lot
where my Tuscan grandfather
had taken your prized possession,

embarrassed to meet the car lot dealer
who wrestled away your T-bird for a song,
and you, still in shock, starting to show.

The empty magnum rested on the floorboard
like a disabled cannon where you sat
disdaining the cold smoke of their voices,

small talk about delivery dates, and you,
only nineteen, still mulling the decision
to be a good Catholic girl and marry the father.

The urge to take over the wheel one more
time and break away, pedal to the floor,
stayed under the surface long after

a choice made in an all-night diner
with a fierce and distant resolve—
I never stopped seeking your love.

SHOTGUN

I drive my son to tee-ball games.
Past the bank where Mom cashed in
our savings bonds for Fruit Loops,
PF Flyers, and Chef Boyardee.

The boy's determined swings
occur a few blocks from where
I was conceived by mistake
in the back seat of a royal blue Thunderbird

near the house where my grandfather
taught me to hit baseballs. He would
sweat into an undershirt and workpants
before the nightshift at Sparrow's Point.

My son swats the ball into a riotous scrum
and tears around the bases, unaware
of his origins, his ancestors,
the trees waving him home.

ONE BLOW OUT THE BRAIN

In memory of Breece D'J Pancake

I found your pages foxed
and yellowed in the used bookstore
summoning me to the shelves.

Those orphaned initials wedged
accidentally between "Breece"
and "Pancake" identical to mine.

Stories "as hard and brilliantly worn
as train rails," wrote Casey.
"Voice of a generation cut short."

Last story finished, I wondered
why you left Reva, Chester, and Colly
to fend for themselves.

We'd met once before, three years
after you killed yourself, my professor
broke down in class,

told us he wanted to eat
your brains for their genius.
The image of you seated outside,

twelve gauge on your lap,
and your phrase—"one blow
out the brain"—stayed with me.

Your ghost came for me that night,
standing over my sleep,
clearing your throat to spit.

You're right,
I never had the guts
to finish the job.

THE WANTING

Daylight spreads
across my floor

like a heroin shot
into the vein. Each breath

wishes for weed.
I twist string beans

the way
I trimmed joints,

guzzle water,
pop aspirin.

The serrated
edge

to slash
my wrists,

skins,
cucumbers.

Lightning flashes
on the crucifix.

A demon walks
out of my dream

across a parquet
floor, puffs

of smoke
from his orange

and bloody
skin rise

through a tunic
of black gauze.

Night
shivers,

I pray

bring God's love,
come rain.

ANYTHING I WANT (HE GIVES IT TO ME)

I bought an eight-ball from a man
in a second-floor walk-up with nothing
but a table, scales, and rock cocaine.

Henchmen filed in and watched him
weigh powder; they scanned me over—
bloodshot eyes wired for killing.

On the street, cold light rising,
I saw a white flash, heard a shotgun
upstairs—started running.

I'd failed out of art school, going nowhere
until the gunshot. I didn't want to die there—
that much, I knew.

PULLING THE TRIGGER

Tulips on a banquet table—
blood orange, succulent—

remind me of you.
Their lustrous cups,

as though rimmed with sugar,
open from silver vases.

I ask a waitress, "Can I take some
back to my hotel room?"

On the road, I want you
close to me.

"Maybe tomorrow," she says.
I consider stealing the vase,

like I did a first kiss
after a botched attempt to show you

the city from my roof.
Your lips never opened.

After you went home, I told myself,
"Next time, no hesitation."

By morning, the flowers
were gone.

PHOTOGRAPH

I found your picture
buried in my armoire:
Nice, 1994.

Stunning, in a low-cut
violet dress like
an abandoned éclair.

I wanted you on the beach,
sand on our skin,
pressed against stones.

You said this was
the only time you'd been happy
in seven years.

Work called you back early.
En route to the airport,
your eyes glistened.

What a beautiful wife
you were.

THE VIEWING

You've come to my mother's house
to pay last respects, to fondle

quilts and caress the furniture
one last time while wishing
our settlement included them.

The deer from the maples
in pairs, the whites of their tails

hurdling through rain after breakfast.
We follow them from the window
without ammunition. Branches slap

the panes. I lay my corpse out to rest
on the chaise and remember how

you came to me in those bluish dawns
like a buck to a salt lick. We melted
the edges round. Shotguns break
our silence. You light votives,
arrange roses, and clasp

my hands together
on the center of my chest,
kneeling down in prayer.

Shotguns boom, unsettling the air
between us. My eyes stay open.

SECRET PLACE

I first thought of kissing you
on the back of a motorbike
in Settignano as we lingered

at the edge of the world,
overlooking the Duomo: ensconced
in late afternoon haze and time:

running late to make the train
from "this little town with beautiful views"
as you scribbled in my moleskin

when we first met. I noticed
your lips at the café—glistening
in the sun from a drink of water,

like *un fiore* after the rain—
and gently held your hips as we entered
your secret place, almost holy,

filled with frescoes of childhood
memories and family outings
underneath the cypress trees—

not to be disturbed by a foreigner
soon headed back across an ocean,
dreaming of home in your arms.

SECOND COMING

We hiked three miles to the Vatican
on the last day of our honeymoon

fully clothed in the heat, dodging
swarms of motor scooters.

I wanted to see Circus Maximus,
Borghese, or Piazza del Popolo.

My first marriage ended in divorce.
I had no business there, though

my mother claims we are related
to Pius XII, "Hitler's Pope,"

the controversial pontiff
who reigned during World War II.

I never believed her.
We lingered at the Pietà,

hooked on to a free tour around the basilica
given by "Sean" from Ireland.

"Glorious," Christina said,
"all this beauty and sin under one roof."

Pius XII wanted his sculpture
to look as mean as possible.

He met with Orson Welles and pumped him
for gossip about the Hollywood stars,

something we do in my Italian family.
I looked closer at his likeness,

his long fingers and treacherous eyes.
He could be one of us.

DELIVERY ROOM

Christina pushed harder in the thirtieth hour,
squeezing my hand as our daughter's blood-flecked head
emerged, and the doctor sliced once at the air for practice,

then lowered the scissors. I looked away at CNN
showing photos of flag-draped coffins for the first time,
snapped on loading docks, air strips, and cargo holds.

Julia spilled into the world, placenta attached,
writhing in the doctor's gloved hands.
In my first official act of fatherhood, I snipped her cord.

Faces from high school yearbooks flashed across the screen:
men and women from Kansas, Oklahoma, and Michigan,
blown from their vehicles, downed in hostile fire,

their shortened trajectories completed in Basra, Najaf, Tikrit—
places their parents would never have dreamed of.
I rock baby Julia in my arms for the first time.

CARDBOARD NOTE

The Polk Street Diner
is closed today

due to the passing
of Miss Annie Mae.

THE LOST PHOTOGRAPHS

Herons captured on a fallen limb
against a backlit grotto of sand,
the blanched light like Monet's

Cathedral at Rouen. I linger there,
clicking off shots, locked into their hunger
like a tabloid photographer.

Next, a texture shot of oyster shells,
dropped through a packing house floor,
left for one hundred years until they rose

out of the water into Avalon Island.
I point my lens, twist the zoom
toward an osprey's shrieking mouth

as she moves closer to her children. And here
on the dock, freshly netted jumbos in peach baskets,
their sea-green backfins half-cloaked in shadow.

Out in my kayak at dusk, I wait for perfect light
to shoot the head of a rockfish as it glints
below the surface, dumbfounded, bodiless.

A bald eagle flashes in the white oaks.
I knock my camera over the gunwale.
The water swallows it whole.

DECOYS

Virginia gentlemen hoist goblets engraved with their names
to the general above the mantle whose portrait signifies
the passage from overalls to starched cotton, savoring
the bourbon as it burns in their throats with a promise
to rise again from the ashes of abandoned plantations.

Cockfights rage off back roads, bloody spurs notch victories
and "good ole boys" fly stars and bars, bathe crosses in kerosene,
seal moonshine in Mason jars as harmless as wooden ducks
on the lake or ghosts of bounty hunters in the dogwood breeze
hunting down slaves, long ago freed, rusted irons in creek beds.

EADY DOES THE EAGLE ROCK

I ate my Nicoise salad
while you stood
for twenty minutes
in the middle of a crowded
dining room, pitched forward,
expectant, beaming

in dreadlocks,
as waiters pretended
you were not there,
like a lilting torchiere
off Michigan Avenue.

One of our nation's greatest
poets, used to this treatment,
even numb to it by now,
still smiling through it all
when I asked the waiter
to seat you. I remembered

the morning you brought
"Jack Johnson Does the Eagle Rock"
into workshop at Virginia,
how you once described
academics in a poem as "fish
stranded in a wheat field."

I should have given
you my table.

LIEUTENANT FOX

You nibbled chestnuts
with *gli partigiani*
and sang "Nearer, My God, to Thee"
after prayers on the terrazzo,
starving until the 92nd came,
two scant platoons.
Mountain villagers hid
from you at first because
they'd never seen Black people.
The soldiers shared rations,
broke bread in the days
before Christmas.
Four hundred Austrian infantry
from the Wermacht division
formed the forward line
of the blitzkrieg offensive
headed for the Port of Livorno.
They infiltrated Sommocolonia
on Christmas Day night.
As dawn broke over the Serchio
Valley, you spied Nazi troops
on the streets below torching houses
where wounded Black G.I.s lay—
shooting as they tried to escape.
You radioed the gunnery
to send up a smoke screen
so your platoons could get out
and then to fire on your position.
"Bring it closer," you ordered

someone who you knew could lay
a mortar on the back of a cat
and he hesitated until you said,
"Fire it." A priest found you
in the rubble of 100 dead Austrians—
you'd slowed their advance,
given the allies a chance
to retake the village.
Fifty years later,
your country
finally gave you
the Medal of Honor.

SOMETHING TO COOL YOU OFF

July, 8, 1944

Saturday afternoon, summer of '44, heat rising
from the Durham tar, Private Booker T. Spicely boarded
a bus, cradling a watermelon for a mother and her son,
strode proudly in uniform into a seat near the front.

The driver, Lee Council, watched him from the mirror,
never said a word until two white soldiers got on, then pointed
to the State Law sign requiring negroes to "sit from the rear,"
and told the Black soldier to move all the way back.

Spicely stood up, smiled, and said, "If I can take a bullet
and die for democracy, I can sit anywhere I damn well please."
The white soldiers nodded, in solidarity, and boldly landed
in the negro section, all the way back, defying the law.

Spicely joined the white soldiers there. Council cursed them all.
Booker T. Spicely struck back, "If you weren't a goddamn 4-F,
you wouldn't be driving this bus." The driver glared
at him and said, "I've got something to cool you off."

Spicely apologized, "I'm sorry, driver, if something I said
may have offended you. I beg your pardon, I didn't mean any harm."
Then he sat on the farthest-back bench for the duration
of his ride, exiting at Fourth and Club Boulevard.

Council watched him disembark and snatched a .38
from under his seat, waited as Spicely came toward the front
of the bus, and shot him point blank in the chest, piercing
his dog tags, and then shot him again, leaving him to bleed to death.

Watts Hospital refused to administer treatment, but they still tested him
for alcohol (the results were negative). Son of Lazarus and Alberta,
born in Blackstone, Virginia, stationed at Camp Butner, Spicely
died upon arrival at Duke Hospital, gunpowder burns on his uniform.

In a crooked scrawl, his death certificate stated "homicide"
from a "pistol shot wound through heart." Council
finished his route, then turned himself in. He was bailed out
that night by Duke Power, which operated the bus concession.

Lee appeared cool and collected as he lied on the stand,
saying his life was in danger: that the Black soldier had reached
into his pocket for an imaginary gun; that the Black soldier
had threatened to cut his throat on previous rides.

Saturday afternoon, summer of '24, heat rising
from the Durham tar, Booker will be eighty years gone—
how much longer will these killings go on? There is no marker
or monument for this fallen Black soldier—just the voices

of witnesses who said he was "shot down like a dog
and left on the ground," and "if a Black man had killed
a bus driver, he would've been lynched by sundown."
In a city once hailed for the taste of its tobacco,

an all-white jury took just twenty-eight minutes to set
Council free and he went back to work the next week.
Private Booker T. Spicely dutifully served our country
against the Nazis—only to be murdered by Jim Crow.

VIRGINIA CREEPER

for Charles Wright

I think of you
endlessly on the move

always something to fleamarket for
in the forest at dusk—

broken manacles in the leaf rust
and fields that murmur on.

Light and its absence enough
to keep you in pursuit of native tongues

flickering outside the skin.
Gather what you can before nightfall—

silence of hawk's eye taking in its prey,
rustle and fire of late August wind.

FATHER'S DAY SHOTGUN SALE

The H&R Pardner
pump action
twelve gauge
shotgun
is the number
one choice
in home
protection
for Coronavirus
at the Dick's
Sporting Goods
in Durham

according
to the sales
associate
because it's
easy to aim
through
doorways
and great
for turning
corners, known
for its smooth
action—
a beast
of a pump
at a beautiful
price

to stave off
home invasion
when days
grow darker
than they are
right
now

.357

Stuffed in his sock drawer and loaded
with hollow points, I wait for him

to tell me what to do. It's been
so long since he's touched me.

I can't even remember how it feels
to fire round after round

at the target. Most of my cousins
are housed in leather holsters

on the belts of police officers,
gangsters, hit men.

He whispers about me in secret,
trots me out to a girlfriend

on the side. I make him
feel good about himself.

His children don't want me.
They hold my nozzle with two fingers

like a piece of soiled laundry.
They believe I'm here to bolster

their father's sexual potency.
He will shoot someone

before it's over.
I will be blamed.

SNIPERS

kiss the bullet,
load it in the chamber.
Squeeze the trigger.

Pick off the easy marks,
spray blood like holy water.
Turn away as targets collapse

into a hunter's landscape.
Terrorize with precision.
Riddle the muse.

SHOOTING GALLERY

I.

The bullet traveled through her brain
like a crystalline thought.

A lunar module careening toward
her skull at high speed,
past rows of breakfast cereals
and condiments and vegetables
and tabloid photos of Lindsay Lohan
and Justin Bieber witnessing the scene
from the Safeway checkout line, muted
and horrific, because the trigger is a trigger
of something deeper and sticky on the inside
and bullets can be served up rapid fire,
quicker than shots of whiskey
for each according to their need.
Automatic weapons kill people
easy, like milk pouring
into a bowl of Cheerios.

II.

The children left Sandy Hook
in bloody clothes, heads down,

eyes closed.

Their dodge ball game over.
The fragile piñatas of their bodies

exploded.

The schoolmates they left behind,
motionless in a sea of finger painting;

and their unopened holiday gifts,
the Wii games, coats, new pajamas,

bicycle and football helmets,
train sets, the unspent

material of their dreams enough to broker
world peace.

The shooter used
the civilian version

of an M-16, the equivalent
of an axe to a sapling—

the death toll rising
from the barbed wire

of his soul. His mother dead.
Children left the school

in bloody clothes.

Is that not enough?

III.

On an early spring morning,
Tec 9s and Glocks ring

like dismissal bells, proving
that automatic weapons can kill

a sample size of thirty-one
students, instructors, and staff,

including the valedictorian,
pre-med major, bong-smoker,

dancer, frat boy, engineer,
linebacker, associate professor,

accountant, dreamer, and their blood
pools in corridors, with shredded

and singed clothes made of khaki,
100% cotton, gingham, polyester,

button-down, matted hair,
bone and brain strafed

across chalkboards—
outlining a new curriculum.

IV.

Every state becomes
a shooting gallery

in a country distracted,
drugged and shot up,

riddled with holes
and no god to speak of,

only white tyrants and kings
losing their grip

and rekindling genocide.
We can run, hide, or defend,

three dismal choices
for lives about to end.

That's all we have
before we get shot?

Nothing but make-
believe and pretend

from the Department
of Homeland Security.

Dance, drop, lie
still on the ground.

Catch the bullets
in your hands.

Throw them back.
Moon the shooter.

Dare him to shoot
you in the ass.

Shimmy, shake,
undulate.

Lobby for a Kevlar
fashion line.

It remains just
as Nikki Giovanni said:

We are all targets.
We are all unsafe.

AMERICA

A new breed of undertakers wielding spatulas—
barbecue loins, racks, shoulders, breasts

for twenty-four hours, and repeat their pledge
to dress the world in corrugated metal,

to rebuild bridges, roads, and water supply
after they have been destroyed. Inflatable

Dick Cheneys mingle like Disney characters.
Javelinas, wild turkeys, and deer scamper

into a ring surrounded by shooters with exactly
two rounds of ammunition, keeping in mind

that safety is a number one concern and money, no object.
Animals collapse in smoky clouds, pronounced dead

from multiple gunshot wounds in a competition where
everyone bags a championship assortment of cutlets,

ribeyes, and t-bone steaks packed in Styrofoam coolers
on doorsteps before families return home.

.45

I stay loaded in the glove compartment
in case something goes wrong
on his weekly errands around the city.
There's been a rash of carjackings
and the movement is gaining steam.
Things have been shaky since the riots of '15
and my owner believes they will be coming for him.
I'm not flashy like other handguns,
just a simple revolver with bullets
in my cylinder. You can fit me
in a tight spot like this hot box
on the passenger side for an element
of surprise at close range. My owner is not
a bad man, just inclined toward freelance
law enforcement, a fan of *The Lone Ranger*,
and afraid that society as we know it is coming
unhinged, and it makes him feel better
to turn the pistol on the target of his anger.
I'm just afraid that I will be used to shoot
an unarmed stranger, and then be blamed,
which couldn't be further from the truth.

YELLOW COAT, MOTORBIKE

He's studied the rosewood bones
of saints in Medici museums

Scaled Giotto's tower
and Brunelleschi's dome

Beheld the prowess of "The David"
at the Accademia dell'Arte

Shot sunset on the Arno
from the Ponte Vecchio

Stood before the Gates of Paradise
at the Baptistry of St. John

But none of it comes close
to touching *il cuore*

di Firenze like this vision
of you in a yellow coat

on a motorbike waiting—
with one hand on the throttle

in front of Santa Maria Novella—
to capture his soul.

MIRAGE

He points a gun
at his family

while they watch
a movie together.

He wonders what
it would be like

to pull the trigger.
To wound his wife,

daughter, and son
for the rest of their lives—

the children curled-up,
clutching a pillow

all night as he did for years
waiting for his mother

to come home. He then
turns the pistol on himself.

FINAL OUT

A wicked sweeping curve
drops off the table and nips
the outside corner unhittable enough
to win you a Cy Young the same year
you outdueled Seaver in old Comiskey

with a beguiling yellow hammer
that twirled from your southpaw fingers
and vanished into the catcher's mitt
as you glared like Wild Bill Hickok
at the batter, hair swinging

under your cap as you punched
them out and years later, looking
clean cut, downcast as you walked
slowly off the mound after getting
the last out at Memorial Stadium.

We never knew about the dark spaces
haunting your retirement, disguised
by a New England wit saltier than a Cape Cod
potato chip, a voice we craved on TV broadcasts
or a front office job that never suited you

as you ran the team after the magic died
on its way downtown and you were cast aside
with your friend Elrod Hendricks
and became despondent because
you were really born to be a pitching coach

and after fourteen years of losing
you started hitting the package goods store
without a clue that everyone knows
what's going on in Baltimore, and people
saw you with pint-sized paper bags.

On a beautiful day for baseball,
a shadow covered the pitching mound
of your soul and you pointed a shotgun
at your face and pulled the trigger.
The former ace of the pitching staff

bleeding out the pain of a losing
franchise onto the withered August grass
and later, your former teammates
paid homage on the broadcast: Jim Palmer
and Rick Dempsey crying on the air.

Your downtrodden Birds, down two outs
in the ninth, came back to defeat the Red Sox
a few weeks later on a miraculous night
only your ghost could have had a hand in:
ousting your childhood team from the playoffs

and your number "46" on a banner just under
the press box that night and at the Legends museum
by the EXIT sign because you left us
way too soon before it all got better
one season later and the team started

winning again on its way to a pennant
and when l think of you on the mound
l hear Chuck Thompson's voice after
you retired the side with a swing and a miss:
"Mike Flanagan... Struck. Him. Out."

THE WRECKING OF OLD COMISKEY

Here's to the Windy City—
built for the freezing of meats,
where Speedway Wrecking,
not Shoeless Joe, is the hardest hitter of all.

In the city of the big shoulders
where bilious aldermen rule,
the wrecking ball stands in the batter's box
smashing old Comiskey down.

The tangled medusa of grandstands
threaten to collapse on the crane,
a screaming liner from Desert Storm
blows the facade away.

This new field of dreams
resembles a Chicagoland mall,
without dolmen or rune,
a merchandise mart for baseball.

Fireworks signal a White Sox victory
and the ruins echo with cheers,
each burst above the silent green seats
a promise of total destruction.

Those large cathedral windows
that once gorged the field with light,
now they're the eyes of Polyphemus—
scorched and vacant ciphers.

When my cleats have reached the warning track,
and my innings are almost done,
I hope heaven is a grand old ballpark
with bleachers in the sun.

MISERICORDIA BLUES

I played a concert for the ghost of my mother
three days after her death in the room
where she lay dying for five days,

watching a death mask slowly overtake
her face with my brother who thought
we'd be laughing about this in a year.

I was afraid to go down to that place
where we spent her final hours in desperate
conversations as her life poured out and she

read us the Riot Act and told us a story about
playing outside the Napoli family bar
as a little girl leaping from stone to stone

up a long hill over strawberries growing wild
between them and allowing herself to eat one
only if she could make it to the top without falling.

I could still see her face on the pillow
against the headboard as she stared up at the ceiling
with her long black hair spilling down around her

and we should never have moved her from that spot
to the hospital for a bag of blood to buy us time
to get her to Milan or Pisa where doctors might explain

what was shutting her body down. But all
I could do for her was sing to the remnants of her soul
in that chamber and share songs that she played

for me as a boy as we sat together in front
of the stereo—ones I knew she loved.
She came with me to buy the guitar in Lucca

before she was sick so she could bring music
for her Italian friends and because I knew it
would sound good there against the ancient stones.

She'd never been to a guitar store in her life.
We had a wonderful time together that afternoon
in Lucca as I strummed the instruments.

Sometimes I cried while singing the songs
because death was not a word I associated with her.
She loved "Bobby Dylan" so I played "Tangled Up in Blue"

and "Forever Young" and Neil Young's
"Cowgirl in the Sand" and "Ambulance Blues"
for the Italian Health Service, with its paramedics

in sky blue and gold Thunderbird suits, who arrived late
on her last day, only to dump her into the chaos
of an emergency room with the word for mercy—

"misericordia"—emblazoned on their truck.
She held my hand and my brother's and said,
"We sure fucked this one up, didn't we?"

WARRIOR

My last photo of you
gazing upward

fear in your eyes
while ruby beads

from a transfusion
drip slowly—

fleeting grains
in an hourglass,

round balls
of buckshot

into my heart.
No food, no water,

no bags of blood
a few days later—

niente.

On your death bed,
life pouring out of you

with your boys
gathered around

the headboard
and you, a long way

from Iris Avenue
in East Baltimore

still worried about who
was going to feed us.

Why do roses die?
Lying in state all day

against your will,
an ancient Italian law

to ensure
that ruin is formal.

I will never forget how
beautiful you looked there

like an Apache warrior
sacrificed to the gods,

all of your weapons at rest
in that moment,

the lightness of you
somewhere above

this open casket moving on,
and the stillness

of hands I will
never hold again.

THREE POEMS OF DEPARTURE ON ROUTE 96

I.

Oxblood sky, snapdragons
on the orchard grass fresh for eating,

I race to catch Joan Baez
at The State and hear her sing

"The Night They Drove Old Dixie Down"
because she reminds me of you

driving a rusted-out maroon Corvair
when that song came on WCAO

when I was six years old in the back seat
playing Barrell Full of Monkeys—

...they never should have taken
the very best.

Upstate New York, two-lane country road
at dusk, a doe to my left bursts

headlong across the crumpled stalks
like a greyhound, hooves aloft,

hellbent on the Prius in front of me;
she glances off the bumper

and soars over my car
in a silent and peaceful arc.

I follow her flight
to the ground—

rippling on impact.

II.

Passing thru Interlaken, all closed up
on Martin Luther King Day,

you on my mind the whole way,
rehashing lines from your note,

trying to diagnose your condition.
The only business in town

marked "open" with a red,
white, and blue banner

unfurling in a squall at dusk
and a spotlight fixed on the sign:

"Guns and Ammo."

You made framed collages
of Dr. King, one with jagged

crêpe paper drops of blood from his head.
I stared at them for hours as a boy.

The last paragraph revealed
a perfect vision of you:

Marching out of the hospital,
mink coat, nightgown, diva shades,

no underwear, tubes still attached,
waving goodbye.

III.

Ghosting drifts rise and dance
on a white gold sheet

untouched at sunset; wisping
torsos and faces swirling

in legions across the road.
This is when I knew.

POEMS IN *BALTIMORE SONS* HAVE APPEARED
IN THE FOLLOWING PUBLICATIONS:

Beltway
  "Bullet Fragments"

Bigger Wednesday
  "Meeting Archie Clark at the Flaming Pit"
  "Misericordia Blues"
  "Gwendolyn and Freddie"

Clash by Night Anthology
  "Anything I Want (He Gives It to Me)"

The Coachella Review Blog
  "Something to Cool You Off"

DC Poets Against the War Anthology
  "America"
  "Delivery Room"

Innisfree Poetry Journal
  ".357"
  "Last Photographs"
  "Pulling the Trigger"
  "Six Shooters" (formerly "My Father's Gun, #3")

Poetry East
  "Cardboard Note"
  "Empty the Chamber"
  "Reading James Baldwin on Election Day in Charleston"
  "Riots"
  "Secret Place"

Smartish Pace
> "Ali"
> "Father's Day Shotgun Sale"
> "Final Out"
> "Howitzer"
> "Photograph"
> "Sportswriter"

Smile Hon You're in Baltimore
> "Trash Night, Guilford"
> "Outlaw"

Upstreet
> "Cash for Guns, 1975"
> "At the Bel-Loc Diner"

Bill Hughes

DEAN BARTOLI SMITH is a published author, poet, and freelance journalist.

His poetry has appeared in *Poetry East, Open City, Beltway, The Pearl, The Charlotte Review, The Cultural Studies Times, Gulf Stream,* and *Upstreet,* among others. His book of poems, *American Boy* (Washington Writers Publishing House, 2000) won the 2000 Washington Writer's Prize and was awarded the Maryland Prize for Literature in 2001 for the best book published by a Maryland writer over the past three years. He is also the author of *Never Easy, Never Pretty: A Fan, A City, A Championship Season* (Temple University Press, 2013).

Smith received an MFA in Poetry from Columbia University in 1989. He is an adjunct professor of publishing in the Masters in Professional Studies program at George Washington University and the director of Duke University Press.

A NOTE ON THE TYPE

The titles of this book are set in New Hero, designed by Mike Newlyn of the brand typography design firm Newlyn. The body text of this edition appears in Calluna, created by Jos Buivenga (exljbris).

This book would not have been possible
without the hard work of our staff.

We would like to acknowledge:

TOMMY SHEFFIELD   Managing Editor
ROSE STRODE   Assistant Managing Editor
VICTORIA MENDOZA   Editorial Assistant
ALEX HORN   Marketing & Media Assistant
LINDA HALL   Operations Assistant

SCOTT BURKE   Publisher
GREGG WILHELM   Editorial Advisor
MEGHAN McNAMARA   Marketing & Media Advisor
DOUGLAS LUMAN   Art Director

STILL
HOUSE
PRESS